Things I Didn't Know How To Say

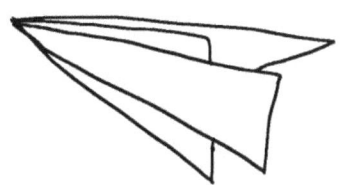

Wendy Rodriguez

To you who reads this;
I hope you find what you're looking for
Even if you don't know what that is yet.

SOMEWHERE

I AM ONE WITH THE UNIVERSE
BUT I AM NOT ONE WITH MYSELF

A COMBINATION OF WORDS III

I WILL STRIKE YOU DOWN
WITH THE LIGHTNING BOLTS
BETWEEN MY THUNDER THIGHS

THE COSMOS

HOW MANY TIMES HAVE I LAID AND WONDERED
ABOUT MY PLACE IN THE UNIVERSE
AND THE UNIVERSE'S PLACE IN ME

I WILL DANCE WITH THE COSMOS
UNTIL WE ARE IN RHYTHM
EVEN IF IT MEANS I WILL DANCE FOR ETERNITY

UNRELIABLE

I FEEL FOR YOU
THE SAME WAY I FEEL TOWARDS MY SHOELACES
WHEN THEY BECOME UNTIED
EVEN WHEN I DOUBLE KNOT THEM

LAMP

YOU ONLY LOVE ME WHEN THE STARS ARE OUT

ARMS

YOU ARE AN OCEAN BIG ENOUGH TO HOLD ME

24/7

I AM DINER SHOP COFFEE
ORDERED AT YOUR CONVENIENCE
HOT OR COLD,
HAVE ME ANY WAY YOU WANT

DINER SHOP COFFEE

YOU CAN HAVE ME 24/7
BUT YOU DON'T

LOSER

I'M NOT GOING ANYWHERE
YOU ARE THE ONLY THING THAT COULD HAVE
BEEN

I'M NOT SURE WHAT TO SAY
YOU HAVE NO CLUE HOW MUCH I LOVE YOU

WITHOUT A DOUBT,
THE MOST BEAUTIFUL THING IS THAT YOU ARE
THE SAME AS THE FIRST TIME

A COMBINATION OF WORDS IV

HOW MANY TIMES DO YOU THINK I CAN GET
AWAY FROM
THE BEGINNING
MIDDLE
AND END?

POLAROID

I'VE PICTURED US TRAVELING ALONG THE COAST
OF CALIFORNIA MORE TIMES THAN I CAN COUNT
IT PLAYS OUT IN MY HEAD, FRAME BY FRAME
LIKE A MOVIE
YOU'LL BE DRIVING AND I'LL BE IN THE
PASSENGER'S SEAT
WITH MY FEET UP ON THE DASHBOARD
YOU'LL BE DRIVING AND I'LL BE IN THE
PASSENGER'S SEAT
THINKING ABOUT HOW I'M GLAD THAT WE EXIST
IN THIS EXACT MOMENT IN TIME
AND HOW THE CHANCES OF THIS HAPPENING
WERE SMALL
I PICTURE US DRIVING UP THE COAST OF
CALIFORNIA
I PICTURE US DANCING WITH THE COSMOS
AND I PICTURE MYSELF LOOKING AT YOU
AND THINKING ABOUT HOW ALL OF THE COLORS
AT THE EDGE OF THE WORLD
MAKE ME FEEL THE SAME WAY YOU DO

AND THEN THE PICTURE FADES,
LIKE A POLAROID IN REVERSE

A DRINK

NOVEMBER BEAT THE BLUE OUT OF ME
AND I WAS MAGENTA UNTIL I WASN'T

DECEMBER HELD A FROSTY FINGERTIP TO MY
COLLARBONE AND POLITELY ASKED,
"MAY I HAVE SOME OF THAT?"

TREE TRUNKS DRAGGED ME THROUGH JANUARY,
WHO SAID
"YOU'D LOOK GOOD ON ME"
TO WHICH I REPLIED,
"OF COURSE I WOULD"

FEBRUARY COATED ME IN AN UNREASONABLE
AMOUNT OF SUGAR
I WAS DRESSED AND OUT THE DOOR BEFORE I
COULD SHIVER

MARCH TOOK ONE LINGERING LOOK AT ME,
TO WHICH I DIVULGED,
"A PHOTO WOULD LAST LONGER,"
TO WHICH,
"SNAP
SNAP
SNAP"

AND TOSSED ME MANGLED INTO APRIL
WHO DUSTED ME OFF AND SAID
"GO GET 'EM TIGER"
AND I RAN AND RAN AND RAN

SMACK!
RIGHT INTO MAY,
WHO APOLOGIZED PROFUSELY

AND I FELL FACE FIRST INTO JUNE,
WHO MADE ME MELT UNDER THEIR SHOES

JULY CAREFULLY UNCURLED MY FIST,
AND THERE,
I HELD MY SADNESS

AUGUST HELD A SHARP FINGERTIP TO MY
COLLARBONE AND WARMLY ASKED,
"MAY I HAVE SOME OF THAT?"
TO WHICH I EAGERLY REPLIED,
"HAVE IT ALL"

I CHOKED SEPTEMBER DOWN LIKE LIQUOR
AND THEY LEFT A BAD TASTE IN MY MOUTH

OCTOBER KISSED ME HOT
AND SLIPPED ITS WICKED TONGUE DOWN MY
WICKED THROAT

STOPLIGHT

EVERY RED LIGHT WE HIT
GIVES ME MORE TIME TO SAY
I LOVE YOU MORE THAN A FRIEND
BUT LESS THAN A LOVER

WHERE IT WAS GOING

I HOPE YOU KNOW
THAT I CAN BE THE PERSON YOU LOVE
AND YOU ARE THE ONLY ONE THAT IS ON MY MIND

I'M NOT GOING TO LET YOU BE MINE
I DON'T WANT TO SEE THE WAY YOU WANT ME

IT WAS REALLY GOOD TO BE ABLE TO SEE WHERE IT WAS GOING
AND IT WOULD NEVER BE

I'M STILL NOT SURE WHAT IT WAS
BUT IT'S OKAY

BELOW

SOMEONE NEEDS TO STOP ME FROM DOING THIS
I ALWAYS HAVE TO WATCH THIS MOVIE

IT'S SO COLD AND COLD AND COLD

BUT I'M STILL WAITING ON YOU
MAYBE YOU WILL BE ABLE TO SEE WHAT I CAN SEE
AND YOU WILL WANT TO HAVE IT

HEADPHONES

WE DON'T HAVE TO TALK ABOUT IT
IT'S OKAY TO BE A ROMANTIC
BUT YOU DON'T WANT TO BE THE FIRST TO
BECOME THE WORLD

I'M GONNA SLEEP WITH MY HEADPHONES ON
AND LET YOU BE ABLE TO MAKE IT MORE
DIFFICULT

THE GAMBLER

I WANT TO BE YOUR FAVORITE WORD

WE ALMOST WERE

YOU SKIPPED THE ROCK AND WATCHED IT SINK

I PLAYED THE GAME AND LOST

CAREFUL

TAKE ME CLUMSY

ANXIOUS

I'M ANTICIPATING YOUR TOUCH LIKE I'M WATCHING A HORROR MOVIE

BLACK COFFEE

I PRETENDED NOT TO NOTICE THE WAY YOU TOOK YOUR COFFEE
I THOUGHT I COULD BE
THE THING THAT MADE YOU A LIGHTER COLOR
A SWEETER TASTE

MOVIE

I SPENT THE WINTER LEARNING ABOUT THE
HUMAN PARTS OF YOU
AND LAUGHING BETWEEN STOP LIGHTS
AND SPENDING HOURS IN THE PASSENGER'S SEAT
LISTENING AND LEARNING AND LOVING EVERY
PART OF YOU
AND I STUDIED THE WAY YOU LOOKED AT ME
WITH EVERY CLUMSY WORD THAT SLIPPED OUT
OF MY STUPID MOUTH
YOU WERE LEARNING, TOO

I SPENT THE SPRING LEARNING TO UNLOVE YOU
AND UNLEARNING TO LOVE THE INFLECTION IN
MY NAME WHEN IT BREAKS THE SEAL BETWEEN
YOUR TEETH
AND LEARNING TO UNLOVE YOUR STUPID SMILE
AND UNLEARNING THE WAY YOU TAKE YOUR
COFFEE
AND LEARNING TO UNLOVE THE WAY YOU LOVE
WHAT YOU DO
AND UNLEARNING TO LOVE THE HUMAN PARTS OF
YOU

TORN

I FOUND YOU IN EVERY LINE I DREW
BUT I COULDN'T BRING MYSELF TO COMPLETE
THE PICTURE

JIGSAW

TELL ME WHAT I WANT TO HEAR
YOU KNOW IT'S NOT A BAD THING
TO PUT THE PIECES TOGETHER

I'M GETTING GOOD AT LETTING YOU WIN
YOU'RE GIVING ME A LOT OF THINGS THAT YOU
DON'T KNOW IF YOU WANT

THE ONLY THING ABOUT BEING THE PERSON WHO
WINS
IS THAT YOU DON'T KNOW HOW MUCH I WANT
YOU TO

CON CUIDADO

I HOPE YOU MISS MY MOUTH
RUNNING
AND
RUNNING
AND
RUNNING

MY FAVORITE MOVIE

WE SAT IN THE DARK AND I WANTED TO TOUCH YOU
BUT I DID NOT KNOW IF I SHOULD

WE LAID ON YOUR SHEETS AND I ASKED ABOUT THE STARS ON THE CEILING
AND FELT THE WAY YOU WERE LOOKING AT ME WITH FEELINGS
I WAS UNSURE IF I WAS TOO CLOSE
OR TOO FAR
YOU CAME CLOSER AND KISSED ME

I WAS ALMOST CERTAIN YOU WANTED TO TOUCH ME
BUT DID NOT KNOW HOW
OR IF YOU SHOULD

THERE ARE TOO MANY THINGS THAT COULD GO RIGHT

THE SAND SLIPPED THROUGH MY FINGERS
I LOOKED AT YOU
THE SUN SET AND I WAS WARM

YOU DROVE IN THE DARK AND I THOUGHT ABOUT HOLDING YOUR HAND
AND HOW EASY IT WOULD HAVE BEEN
IF I HADN'T BEEN SO SCARED

STANDING ON PEBBLES
I WANTED TO KISS YOU
MY COURAGE SEEPED INTO THE SOIL
I WALKED BACK INTO THE HOUSE

THE LATE MORNING CAUGHT ME IN SHAMBLES

I WROTE WHAT I WANTED TO SAY
INSTEAD OF LETTING THE WORDS STUMBLE OUT
OF MY MOUTH

I BRACED MYSELF FOR WHAT I KNEW WAS
COMING
I LOOKED AT MY SHOES
I LET MY BREATH BE HEARD

THERE ARE TOO MANY THINGS THAT COULD GO
WRONG

OLD HABITS

I SPENT A MONTH MAKING FAKE LOVE WITH SOMEONE
WHO WASN'T SURE OF THE WAY IN WHICH THEY WANTED ME

I'M STILL NOT SURE IF I'M SOMEONE I CAN LOVE

YOU STAYED THE SAME SAME SAME
AND YOU'RE STILL WATCHING THE SAME STUPID MOVIE
AND LETTING SOMEONE WHO DOESN'T KNOW IF THEY COULD LOVE YOU
MAKE FAKE LOVE TO YOU

WHITE SANDS

DON'T LOOK AT ME LIKE YOU KNOW I'M IN LOVE
WITH YOU
YOU KNEW HOW TO KILL ME
ONE WORD AND I'M OVER YOU
ONE LOOK AND
I'M NOT SO SURE THAT I CAN PRETEND
YOU HAVEN'T BEEN LIVING IN THE BACK OF MY
MIND

ONE LOOK AND I'M YOURS

THE LOVELIEST LIES OF ALL

I FOUND PLASTIC FLOWERS IN MY RAINCOAT AND
I PLANTED REAL ONES IN PLACES YOU COULD FIND
IF YOU WERE LOOKING
MUDDY BOOTS FOLLOWED ME INTO PLACES I DIDN'T WANT YOU IN

THE PLACES I USED TO FIND YOU ARE NOW
PLACES YOU HAVE NEVER BEEN

I HAVE MISSED YOU FOR THE LAST TIME

TINY SHADOWS

THE ANTS IN MY KITCHEN
STILL BOTHER ME LIKE A BAD MEMORY

HOW DO I KNOW THAT THE THING THAT I'M KILLING
ISN'T SOMETHING I'VE SEEN BEFORE

BEING BRAVE IS EASY IF YOU JUMP BEFORE YOU CAN FEEL IT

I CAN'T TELL IF I'M SCARED ANYMORE

HANGING IN A MUSEUM

IT IS BOTH THE WORST AND BEST THING
TO LOVE SOMEONE

CLIFFS

I BECAME MORE OF MYSELF FROM KNOWING YOU

BOBBY PINS

YOU KNOW WHERE TO FIND ME
IN THE SPACE BETWEEN YOUR FINGERS
IN PHRASES INFREQUENT AND FAMILIAR

EL DESCUBRIMIENTO

I HAVE FOUND
THAT ALL THE RIGHT THINGS
ARE THINGS I DIDN'T KNOW HOW TO SAY
AND MAYBE IF I HAD TRIED
I WOULD HAVE FOUND WHAT I WAS LOOKING FOR

INSTEAD,
I FOUND A PLACE TO LET YOU KNOW
THAT I AM THINKING ABOUT YOU
ON A PAGE YOU WILL NEVER SEE
IN A LINE YOU WILL NEVER READ
FROM A PLACE YOU WILL NEVER HAVE KNOWN

www.ingramcontent.com/pod-product-compliance
Lightning Source LLC
LaVergne TN
LVHW052258070426
835507LV00036B/3385